SAY IT HURTS

LISA SUMME

SAY IT
HURTS

YESYES BOOKS PORTLAND

COVER & INTERIOR DESIGN: ALBAN FISCHER

ISBN 978-1-936919-86-4
PRINTED IN THE UNITED STATES OF AMERICA
LIBRARY OF CONGRESS CATALOGING-IN-PUBLICATION
DATA IS AVAILABLE UPON REQUEST.

PUBLISHED BY YESYES BOOKS
1614 NE ALBERTA ST
PORTLAND, OR 97211
YESYESBOOKS.COM

KMA SULLIVAN, PUBLISHER
STEVIE EDWARDS, SENIOR EDITOR, BOOK DEVELOPMENT
ALBAN FISCHER, GRAPHIC DESIGNER
COLE HILDEBRAND, SENIOR EDITOR OF OPERATIONS
ALEXIS SMITHERS, ASSISTANT EDITOR
PHILLIP B. WILLIAMS, COEDITOR IN CHIEF, VINYL
AMIE ZIMMERMAN, EVENTS COORDINATOR

For Sara, of course.

Contents

You, the moon. You, the road. You, the little flowers
by the side of the road.

—RICHARD SIKEN, "Road Music"

Light as a Feather   Stiff as a Board

When we played it   at a sleepover   Jackie's house

       fifth grade   It worked   Five girls held me

up to the ceiling in the foyer   with only

       their pointer & middle   fingers our hands

so lesbian   all of our ring fingers   longer than

       our indexes   Some of us knew what lesbians

were then   but didn't know   the finger thing

       No one accused me   of admiring   of looking

of loving   of anything   I put on my pajamas

       in the bathroom tried not to notice

anyone's bra   stayed in my own sleeping bag

       I had heard the name   Matthew Shepard

When you are   queer

there is always violence   I always think

violence   intrusive as acne then   I was in love

with Liz that year   no   maybe

it was Alyssa   When a lesbian   writes a poem

it's a lesbian poem

Our Dream Wedding

One day in math class I plotted our dream wedding on a sheet of graph paper from my graph paper notebook. It was the first time I ever thought about getting married. You had no idea that I wanted to marry you & maybe it was because we were just ten years old. I would say that's too young for girls to be thinking about getting married but the truth is that girls that young are thinking about getting married. The church & the cross on top of the church were very easy to draw with all the squares & since I was a kid when I planned our dream wedding I still believed in church. That church was where everyone got married. What I liked about you was that you always shared your Dunkaroos with me. My mom barely got us Dunkaroos because they cost too much. You only liked the cookies so I got to have all the frosting to myself which was good because there wasn't really enough of it for all the cookies. In the drawings both of us were rectangles. You were eleven squares tall & just right & I was only eight squares tall because I was really short as a kid. You had these beautiful curls in real life that I unfortunately had to straighten in our dream wedding because of the straight lines on the paper & because I'm a perfectionist. It bothered me that on the page certain things didn't look right. Like how the flowers in your hand were just squares on sticks. I tried to make up for things not looking right by drawing hearts all over to add to the romance of it but they ended up looking half like field goal posts & half like bad drawings of Ohio. Luckily holding hands on the page was easy besides the fact that we didn't have fingers because having fingers on graph paper looked like Wolverine claws which I did not like & so erased. I'd always wanted to hold your hand for about three weeks before our dream wedding & this was where it happened. What was dreamy about our dream wedding was the palm trees next to the church. I knew we were in Ohio but in a dream wedding anything can happen. The coconuts on the palm trees were square but you could still tell what they were. I wore a top hat because that was easy to draw & it just made more sense to me if one of us was the boy because at the time I didn't know about lesbians. I liked to do boy things like play baseball & swing sticks like swords in the woods so I didn't see why I couldn't be the boy for you. The limousine ride was going to be the best part. It was a big rectangle that looked a lot like us but sideways. The wheels were square like everything else which was just one of the reasons why it never went anywhere.

The first time I French kissed you

was the same as the first time I kissed a girl
the same as the first time I kissed anyone.
My tongue in your mouth like a promise. During high school
sleepovers we only invited each other. We brushed our teeth
for whole minutes, did not understand why our underwear was wet.
We knew what lesbians were only in the context of high school
social hierarchy & Catholicism. *We are not lesbians*
we said to each other. We didn't have cell phones
to say *meet me here* but we met in the locker room
before third bell. There was no second bell gym class.
There was no second chance for me when you lit a cigarette
in the movie theater parking lot, said it differently
I am not a lesbian.

Coming Out

I drive an hour to your apartment, having only met you once,
shook your hand at a party in Cincinnati where we got drunk

on shitty Long Islands & inched our way back to a bedroom
where we made out for hours, clawed at something muscle-deep

in each other in an effort to rescue whatever was inside us—
part brick & mortar, part electric shock, whatever should have been

holding us together. Tonight we pregame at your place with your friends
who don't know you're into me, think you're working on it with Dwight,

Halloween-themed drinks spread across your kitchen counter,
the vodka & fruit punch a little too pink to be violent,

the candy corn martinis little sunrises in our hands. We catch
a ride to a haunted maze, cram into the backseat of Jasmine's Civic,

the collar of your Dracula cape jabbing my jawline,
small space necessitating our touching. In the maze

we run off immediately, find the dark space behind a haystack,
a soft white sheet—someone's abandoned costume—

which we smooth out in tandem with our breath,
your head on my chest the possibility of our new hearts

as wingspan, as what can only carry, glide, fly.
We touch with the intensity of the strangers we are,

but with the tenderness of reuniting,
as if we've missed each other all along.

Poem in Which I Imagine My Dad Agrees to Shave My Head

when he asks / why / i say because / i'm out of money / because i know /
there's a shoebox in the garage / with a pair of clippers inside / santa brought
him / that he hasn't used since / we were kids / my parents couldn't / afford
haircuts for four of us / so my dad learned how / to do it we'd sit outside /
in a row of lawn chairs / he'd move down the line / buzz my brothers' heads
with a #2 / wet our hair before trimming / mine & my sister's bangs / straight
across / so slowly / so carefully / so no one would know / we were getting
backyard haircuts / from our dad / when he finished / he'd gather up our
hair / spread it in his garden / keep the deer / away from his tomatoes / i'm
no longer ashamed / of being poor / late twenties / still in school / never had
a job that paid much / more than minimum wage / when i imagine my dad /
agrees to shave my head / what i mean is i can remember / the love inside my
father / but can no longer / see it / when i was a kid / we tossed baseball / built
birdhouses he hung / in the trees / in elementary school / my best friend asked
me / did i have a mom / when i imagine my dad / agrees to shave my head /
he doesn't ask if / it's a lesbian thing / doesn't tell me / what is "natural" / how
i should be / sorry / instead / he understands this haircut / from an economic
perspective / a buzz will look good / for months even / after it's grown out /
means fewer minutes / spent in a great clips / fewer dollars spent on what / he
can do himself / this is okay / with me he is / a businessman after all

Coming Out

You are a part of nature & nature has no preference.
—Kaitlin, Hot Yoga instructor, Cincinnati, OH

There's that story some parents tell their kids,
that if you return a fallen bird to its nest,

it will be abandoned because the parents can smell you.
This logic denies birds' innate desire to care

for their young & the fact that birds feel most
threatened by what they see. I could feel

my father's eyes on me as soon as I got out of the car
for my grandfather's funeral last May—

my tie, my chinos, my wingtips—his discomfort
his disgust, why'd I want to *look like a man.*

Standing next to him at his father's gravesite,
he put his hand on my shoulder, best he could do

to comfort either of us, unaware
he is both nest & hawk, had always been.

When I built up the courage, years ago,
to tell him I love women, he said *you did not*

choose this, said *never ever touch*
a woman. This is your cross to bear.

For Christmas that year he got me a catechism.
Homosexual persons are called

to chastity. If death
cannot soften my father, I do not know

what can. Return a bird to its nest
& it will be fed as if it was never gone.

Selfie With Straight Girls

Straight girls won't admit it
when they like me, won't say a word
out loud outside of the bedroom
but they'll run their fingers down
my jawline, my chest, my stomach—
I'm constantly flexing my abs
for moments like this—
in a dark corner of a dive bar
while they tell me how
the baseball game ended,
how sunburnt they got in Florida,
look up into my eyes
& hold my gaze the same way
they'll hold me later—forever
until further notice. The few
times I am alone with them
they'll offer me a Bud Light
& hold my hand on the back porch
only after dark, take me
upstairs to their bedrooms
only when their roommates are out
of town, go down on me only under
the bubbling of fish tanks,
the buzz of refrigerators,
as if such background noise
could cover up how my moans

sound so much like theirs.
When I call them
because now I want to take them
out, maybe to the movies,
they don't answer.
When they call back,
days later, they're drunk,
they're in a fight with their sisters
or their mothers,
they haven't seen their fathers
in over a decade, god
they feel so alone, & I pick up
at 3:00 AM on a Monday,
wanting so badly to shove
their troubles under my bed
while I tuck them into it,
if only to hold them there,
listen to the rise & fall
of the tiny storms in their chests,
if only to say *baby, I'm here,*
until morning,
if only they'd stay that long,
if only they'd shown up at all.

Coming Out

I didn't really / learn what bisexual was / until college / part Intro to Women's
Studies textbooks / part kissing girls with boyfriends / the books spit out
/ words like fluid & continuum / & the girls were the kind / who wavered /
between me & their boyfriends / between my bedroom & the homecoming
court / wanting so badly / to be queen / I crowned every single one

those girls / never claimed it but I did / told my friends I was bi / knowing I
wasn't / just wanting some shot at normalcy / but I knew it / was a half-court
shot at the buzzer / could only end / with a groan from the crowd / when the
ball ended up nowhere / near the basket

I went out with boys sometimes / feminist boys / boys who loved books / boys
who could cook / to make sure I wouldn't / learn to like them / I never more
than / made out with a few of them / awkward / movie theater / backseat
events / always ending / in thank yous / brisk walks / up to my bedroom /
never texting them back

after I moved out of my parents' house / I wrote my dad / a letter as a twenty-
first birthday / gift to myself / not saying / bisexual / but gay / a more correct
word then / I left it on his desk / but felt obligated / to call him in the dark /
twist of my panic / warn him what / he'd come home to

when he answered / I said it / gay / he said Jesus / said Merry Christmas / asked
why / it couldn't wait / why / I needed / to tell him / right then / while he was

driving / home from work in a snowstorm / but all I could do was / listen / to him breathe into the phone / relieved I had a father / who answered when I called / I let our silence sit / there my refusal / for once / to apologize

I'm Sorry I Cannot Attend Your Party

It's not your taste for cheap beer
or the fact that your couch smells like boys.
It's not the way your little cat gets stoned by accident
or that at your same party last summer

someone barfed on my new green shoes.
It's not because I know that this time
there will be no piñata because right now
you're really into being an adult.

I'm the drying grass in the hottest summer yet
& you're the sprinkler that only works on the weekends.
I'm the kid with the broken telescope,
just a little dot on this planet,

& you're that big beautiful moon.
I can only look at you from here.

Selfie With What Is & What Is Not

It is so sudden: the way we are:
so warm in this cold:
the ice in our hair melting: running
down our faces: matting us down:
not to be confused with tears:
we can hardly talk: the numbness:
our jaws: our hands: feeling more
than hands: more than my body
& your body pressed together:
I hold you: somewhere:
between what is & what is not:
somewhere: between me & this tree:
a night like this: up against
everything: we smoke cigarette after cigarette:
strike enough matches to melt away
whole blocks of this street: beneath the ice
is everything: the gravel: we try
to anchor our boots in: try to steady ourselves
against anything with a heartbeat: a pulse

Our Lot

Maybe it won't always be here, in my car,
outside of the liquor store, or here, in my car,
in this cul-de-sac, or here, in a secret parking lot,
near, but not too near, a secret hotel

where I drove out too far on purpose,
where there was just enough light to see your eyes
& just enough dark for this to last
more than a few minutes.

But you said it's always going to be here,
in my car. It's always us in the car.
I said maybe not. Maybe I'll know you
in a place much more or much less dangerous

than here in my car, here, in my arms.
That backseat sanctuary.
I could find your hair there.
How you smell. How we could bruise again

& not be sorry for the parts that fit
back there, the parts that are touching.
I'll just keep kissing you like this is it,
like our hearts won't hurt in an hour.

Selfie in the Boys Department

It's awkward. Me, a grown woman,
flipping quickly through the boys' shirts
at Gap Kids, fearing any interaction

with any employee, like the blonde woman
behind the counter, hair pulled back in a tight bun,

who I imagine is uncomfortably aware
that I am not a kid, not a boy,
though definitely too young &/or dykish

to be shopping for her own sons, which is all true,
& in some ways, I am the child,

the little boy I resemble, unable to commit
even to taking this
green plaid shirt or that navy blazer

into the fitting room, fearing the way
the fabric will stretch across my hips & chest,

the way my waist will fail
to fill out the rest of the shirt,
an emptiness so much deeper

than the 50/50 cotton blend
I will not stagger awkwardly

up to the register to purchase,
take home with me, & immediately
google various ways to shrink clothing.

Instead, my bow ties will hang
side by side in the darkness

across the back bar of my closet,
little stars set against nothing,
no sky to be noticed in,

nothing else for me to wish for.

No I Cannot Have Anything

Here is a memory of my father
long before I ever heard
the word *republican*.

He swims freestyle
with me side by side
until I am perfect.

When he buys me ice cream,
I feel his love, not wind.
I cry every time

I read Brokeback Mountain.
My father is not exactly
a violent man. He wouldn't

drag a queer around
by their dick, but he might
watch. He might whisper

faggot. I have his eyes,
not the color but the shape,
downturned, sad. My father

said I can have anything
if I work hard enough.
My father told me women

in men's clothes are distracting,
that I am not a man.
I am not a man.

Always a Man

I am not the kind of woman
whose boyfriend asks
in the midst of all of the sexual assault on the news
how many times in a year
do you think you get catcalled
I do not have a boyfriend first of all
but even if I did my answer would not be
that of my coworker or sister or best friend
incalculable
like the number of times in a year I stub my toe
I am not the kind of woman who looks like a woman
not the kind of woman a man whistles at near the gas station
or calls honey at the bank
or tells to smile because I've got a pretty smile
at the farmer's market
the Jiffy Lube
the coffee shop
the bar down the street
my own porch
because the upstairs neighbor
the mailman
I am not the kind of woman my exes are
women who got hit on right in front me
while I held their hands at the gym or at the movies
or at the fucking Olive Garden
I am not the kind of woman

who has to use her energy to politely decline these advances
or gets called *bitch*
or gets a bloody lip
or gets it anyway
but there is always a man
while I walk home from work
in a button down & bow tie in broad daylight
there is always a man on the corner by the CVS
a man wearing a hardhat on the corner of Bayard St.
there is always a man
who wants to put me in my place
I see what you really are under there he says
you're a girl

Selfie as a Dyke

The problem with being a dyke
is standing in front of your mirror,
naked, feeling both admiration & shame
for the woman in front of you,

who locks eyes with you, looks you up & down,
& walks away. The problem
with being a dyke is the glances you get
in the women's room on a Monday morning

in your office building, on a Friday night
at the local bar, your local bar, where you drink
vodka sodas, play "Cowboy Take Me Away"
on repeat, throw darts. The problem

is the double takes you catch sight of
while you wash your hands, your eyes darting
like a pinball—you do not want women to feel
unsafe, to feel like you're looking at them

the way men look at them, because they can tell
you're a dyke, which is much different than a man,
but you can see it in their faces like a headline,
as strangers consider *should I be afraid?*

Do you belong here? You do.
You tell yourself you do because you do.
Your girlfriend shaves your head,
& though you are sometimes mistaken for a boy,

you are still a woman, just a different kind,
a dyke, a word you are
still deeply uncomfortable with.
The problem with being a dyke is men,

is your father, who you text once in a while
because he's your father & you want to like him,
so you try to talk about "safe" topics with him,
the weather in Pittsburgh vs. the weather in Cincinnati,

your promotion at work, but then he'll say something
unrelated to the rain or your administrative responsibilities,
tell you to vote for T***p, that you're a challenge
but he won't give up on trying

to undo what your liberal arts education did to you,
because you still come from a Good Catholic Family,
& you still have Good Catholic Parents,
& it is at this point you realize here is another

poem about your father, his mouth
unable to say the word *daughter*.

Home for Christmas

for every comment / my father doesn't make / about my body / he throws / two temper tantrums / why isn't aunt mary bringing the mashed potatoes / why is the oven still on / all directed at my mother / rockin' around the christmas tree / punching back at their voices / my mother walks upstairs / we sit in the bedroom she leant me / her bedroom / she says *sorry* / i say *no* / *i'm sorry* / a sorry-fest / as usual / women who have done nothing wrong / my father drives me / in silence / to the bakery that night to get bagels / prepare for christmas morning tradition / asks me every year / *do you eat bagels* / milk jug luminaries for miles / all i can think / is how many cows have suffered / nothing is beautiful / for every thing / a light can show you / my father in the kitchen / making me / a separate vegan coleslaw / his hands calloused & cracked / massaging the oil & vinegar into the cabbage / never laid his hands on my mother / it's been exactly ten years / since he told me / what to do with mine / *never ever touch a woman* / i cannot unhear it / cannot unsee his stiff body / arms crossed / guarding the kitchen sink / from what / *well how do you know you're gay* / i guess i haven't forgiven him / but am trying / for every thing / a light can show you / it contorts two / maybe / because of how i want / things to look / the light / smooths over the way he asks me / via text / to go to mass with him / shushes his politics / lights making him / shiny / so i let them

Coming Out

When I walk into church,
my hands fold automatically.
There is a certain intimacy
you can have with yourself
just by touching your own hands.
When I finally understood worship,
I understood worship.
It became tangible. It was soft
& easy. It became bodies.
There is something reverent
about being on your knees & so I will
always pull a girl closer to my face
by her thighs. I will always
think this is the right thing.
I am always here by accident.
A wedding. A funeral.
When I told my father I love women,
he gave me a catechism,
told me *god loves the sinner*
but not the sin.
When my best friend got married,
I gave her a high five
as she walked down the aisle
& out the back of the church
with her new husband.
Which is to say our hands touched.

At my grandfather's viewing,
I traced the veins of his hand with my fingers
to keep from crying, traced my memory
to his backyard, the swing set,
where, as a kid, I asked god to please
make me into a boy
so that I could marry Lindsey.
Some people go to church
because they're sorry.
I am always here by accident.
Some people get on their knees
when they apologize, push
their hands together in hopes of forgiveness.
I am on my knees & this is no apology.
I am on my knees & my hands are full.

Elegy

I bring you lunch / up to school / unannounced / Panera broccoli cheddar soup
/ with a baguette / Caesar salad / your favorite an apple / because you're / the
teacher / you fuck me in the basement / faculty bathroom / we arrive late to
any party / we were fucking / step out to fuck / in the car my knee knocking
your / stick shift / perpetual bruise / you come / home early from wherever
to / fuck me on the counter / I moved / the clothes from the washer to the
dryer / fuck me in the shower / I went across town / to get your favorite /
hummus when our store was out / fuck me in the backyard / I got the bills
out of the mailbox / filled it with Laffy Taffy / you like the jokes / fuck me
in the doorway / before my job interview / fuck me when I didn't / get a job
/ when eventually I got a job / now I can't / think of the last time we did it /
anywhere but the bed / tonight you're too tired / for the nineteenth night in
a row / you're sorry / your back hurts / you didn't sleep well last night / your
students are assholes / your dad / drank himself into / the hospital / again I'm
sorry / I'm being / insensitive / can't help but know / how many days it's been /
all I want / the familiar unfamiliar / to drink a Smirnoff Ice with you / smash
/ open a piñata with you / go down on you rush / of riding a bike / downhill

Elegy

I.

We buried your dad on a Friday. No, a Saturday. I'm not sure. No, not buried.
Cremated. But first they brought his body to the church. During the service
I sat in the front row between you & your brother-in-law. I was your family
then. Can you tell where this is going? Afterwards, the boys carried the casket
down the aisle & out the back door. We followed right behind them, couldn't
get close enough. I held your hand for the second- or third-to-last time. It
was our last moment with his body, which was hidden, closed up, packaged
away. His skinny legs. His perpetual sunburn. His pastel tank top. No, he wore
a suit to the funeral. The same one he wore to the viewing the night before.
The same one all the boys were wearing. They hoisted him into the back of a
big car. Another thing to leave.

II.

Now just ashes for the river he'd want them in. Now, at twenty-four, both
of your parents dead. I pretended to cough to cover my sobs. It was winter
& everyone was coughing. It was a funeral & everyone was sobbing. It was
Christmas Eve. No, that was the day he died. It was a few days later. Your
sister's voicemails on our phones that morning whole minutes of crying & I
had to wake you. You were tired. You were hungover. *You need to call your sister.*

III.

We were at a wedding the night before, our first & last together. We posed in front of a Christmas tree done up in gold. Your dress, all black, lace. I wore a black tie. We kissed under mistletoe. We had started fixing our problems. I had started writing lines from our favorite poems on napkins & slipping them into your lunch bag & you had stopped telling me that I didn't give a shit. It was going to work out. It was. We were going to have pancakes & morning sex. We were going to exchange just one gift.

IV.

We rushed to Dayton. We smoked pot in your sister's garage, picked at our grilled cheese sandwiches. The first time I met your dad, the first time you brought a girl home, the first thing he said to me: *wanna go out in the garage & smoke pot or somethin'?*

V.

We watched your little nieces open gifts the next morning. *Merry Christmas!* they screeched. *Where is Grandpa Fred?* We went to Kohl's a few days later, returned the pajamas we picked out, the dress shirts. We opened the gifts from your dad that his girlfriend brought over. I kept the PacSun gift card in my wallet for two years, eventually bought a pair of mint colored pants you would've liked.

VI.

What I remember all these years later is the viewing. His high school picture on display. I saw you in there. His eyes so blue, they were almost clear. Your eyes that same blue, made my chest tight in math class all those years ago in college, I grew used to. I am sorry for every way I grew used to you. Tonight & every Christmas Eve I re-watch the In Remembrance slideshow your sister posted to YouTube. I owe you these tears, at least.

VII.

So many pictures. Your sister as a baby on his lap in the corvette. You & Fred in front of your Mazda. You are sixteen & beautiful. Fred in the garage. Fred the mechanic. Fred put a new bumper on my car after someone wrecked into us one rainy Saturday morning when you were driving me to work. I run my fingers across that bumper after every wash & it's smooth like a stone, like your hands.

VIII.

Fred & your mom. I never got to meet her. Fred & your mom holding baby you. Baby Fred. Eighth-grade Fred. Your nose just like Fred's, that same little bulb. Your lips curl at the left corner too when you first begin to smile. Your arms around his neck in the front yard before the prom. Your boyfriend, Andrew. What boy will take care of you when I leave you weeks later?

IX.

Fred fishing. Fred winning a prize, holding up his forty-pound catfish in the seventies. Fred taught you to fish. You taught me to fish the day after we first slept together. The first time we slept together was in Fred's bed. It was your twenty-second birthday. An entire wall of his bedroom was rifles behind glass cases, & I listened to their silence all night. He stayed at his girlfriend's that weekend, said *no boys in my house.*

X.

Fred toasting to his buddies at a cookout, big fat burgers on a round charcoal grill. Fred drinking. After the funeral, everyone from church drank whiskey shots at Tony's. Fred drinking. You wouldn't do it because you hate whiskey. Same. But I drank for both of us.

XI.

Fred on a motorcycle, shock of white hair in the wind. Fred's hair that white for years. Fred young & handsome. Front yard, bellbottoms, no shirt. Fred flexing behind a ping-pong table. Fred kissing your cheek in his kitchen. Me kissing your cheek in our kitchen. You & Fred on the couch in his living room. You & me on the couch in our living room. You could have any girl you wanted.

I look for you

in every stick shift, in every pre-1999 Mazda Protégé,
in every Ford because you just got a brand-new Ford,
an SUV in fact, you've always wanted one,

it's an automatic, & so I automatically look for you
in all the cars on all the roads, because maybe
you're in some Volvo or some Chevy, you could be

a passenger, you could be in a backseat with some guy's
hand on your leg, his tough-guy wallet on a chain,
his blond beard, his tattoos, his kids. I look for you

in our neighborhood even though you moved away,
in the movie theater we went to Tuesday nights,
where my arm lived around your shoulder,

our bodies so close that we knew
holiness, two becoming one,
before we ever took off our clothes. I look for you

on the street you don't live on anymore,
by the fire hydrant your dog loved to shit next to,
in your gravel driveway, the pebbles I dig around in, in case

there's any trace of you, maybe a bobby pin, an earring,
a Wintermint Orbit wrapper, glitter. I look for you
in the chili parlor down the street we only went to

when we were drunk, on the sidewalk outside its entrance,
in the broken beer bottles, the cigarette butts that could be
yours, their lipstick-stained filters I bend down to touch,

to know your mouth again.

Elegy

For Jody
September 22, 1956 – January 13, 2007
& For Caitlin

I. *I never got to meet your mom*

already three years dead
  by the time you sent me that text
you were mine first
that first night I left your place
post-pizza pub
post-holding each other's eyes
  too long to keep calling it friendship

II. *the first time I took off your shirt*

there they were
her initials
JMV in cursive
on your inner right breast
beneath a small cross
  with a pink ribbon wrapped around it
which I later learned was placed exactly
  where her cancer first appeared
even as my tongue traced your tattoo
I grieved her
a stranger

recognizing you are what is left
        of a whole other person
& I missed her for you
a twenty-one-year-old who
more desperately than I understood then
needed her mom

III. *in the letter you wrote me after I left you*

you point to my mother
your first time meeting her
that humid Mother's Day
spring of our senior year
you point to her kindness
how it reminded you of what you didn't have
would never have again

IV. *I did so much wrong when we were together*

failing not just to scoop the litterbox
& talk to you about how I worried
        you didn't love me enough
but to ask you about her
not just build you a tunnel
but shine in a light at the end
show you an outlet
an opening
but I was too afraid to trigger
        the chemo
the baldness
the hospice

the gravestone
the exact words you needed
      to hear from your own mouth
in order to forgive me for never asking

v. in the letter you said we were doomed from the start

when she died, part of me did too
but that I couldn't have known
& you never grieved
but tried to go back to her instead
whole days in the park off Tipp-Cowlesville
dozens of pastries from that bakery in Vandalia
hitting up your high school boyfriend
needing so badly someone
      who knew & loved her
trying to reconnect with her through him

VI. *a love as likely as a flame in a flood*

by the time you got to me
I had a lighter & old newspaper
I had a tent
but Caitlin
the storm
we so quickly became wet kindling
unable to undrown

VII. *the Race for the Cure photos*

I see today on Facebook
remind me of the cold October morning in 2012
my first race
you stayed in bed with a sore throat
I went downtown alone
your absence from the race
        not just one less cheerleader
my absence from the bedside
        not just something better to do but

VIII. *a picture of what we'd become:*

a polished wood frame with crisp matting
but nothing inside
I was running for you
for your mom
as if it could bring us back
        to a time when you might've been in the crowd
as if my sore legs over a 6.2-mile stretch
        were a type of giving or forgiveness
as I neared the finish line
I looked for you anyway
kept running

The Place Where I Again Think of You

Take me back to stumbling uphill
to your Wheeler Street apartment,

to all the times we were just about drunk,
just about to kiss—were this close.

Take me back to splitting my foot open
on that Bud Light bottle & you

Steri-Stripping it shut for me
on your kitchen table. Please, take me back

to bare feet & cold marble tile, to your shower,
to you rubbing my face with menthol

face wash, to us facing each other.
Take me back to your fluffy white towels

right out of the dryer, to the lavender fabric softener
that made me spin inside, to moving in together,

the bliss of that, love on the counter,
love against the wall, love again & again

in the shower, love on the back porch,
love in & of our very own driveway.

Take me back to *Lars and the Real Girl*
on the couch, to my mouth, to your mouth,

to our loft bedroom, where we fought
then fucked to fix it,

to a time when that actually worked.
Please, just take me back

to bed, to the flowered sheets, your legs
wrapped around my waist. Take me back

to little whispers of breakfast,
to our bodies keeping us

in the bedroom, our hunger
the lock on the door.

I find you

in the shower curtain liner, where my darkest hairs might be
your lightest, in those Matisse prints we got at the CAC,
you in a room full of flowers, you playing the violin

naked. I find you in the kitchen, in the measuring spoons,
in the dish rag, the steel-cut oats clogging the drain.
I find you in the junk mail on top of the microwave,

in the ad for the pizza window I eat at when I'm drunk
& when I'm sober. I find you at my desk, in the C-shaped
Post-it notes, in the pink uni-ball pens. I find you on the Internet,

& maybe I was looking there, maybe I googled you,
which is not what I meant to write about, but I find you
there in the three-day detox guide on Pinterest, in the tweet

where you announce Boyz II Men is coming to Cincinnati,
in your dad's ex-girlfriend's new relationship status on Facebook,
I loved her when you didn't. I find you in the box

of us I shoved under my bed, & when I reach back there,
I find you in the mixtapes, the movie ticket stubs,
the boarding passes & seashells, the grit

of the sand in their ridges. I find you in the picture frame,
picture turned around, now just the inscription,
I like the way you look at me.

Friday Night Selfie

When I have cash for ice cream sandwiches at the gas station. When you say thank you. When I kiss you on the neck. When we drink a shot of whiskey. When it's Friday night & fuck am I lonely. When we kiss harder. When your back scrapes the brick on the side of the only movie theater in town. When we get to your father's house. When I think what would your father think. When I think of my own father. When I think if your father is anything like my father he'd. What. When I think. When we get to your father's house. When we lie down on the cool basement tile. When I eat you out. When we don't talk about sad things like how chickens are raised or the exes we're still in love with. When you're just the girl I'm looking for. When your teeth are smooth like the inside of seashells. When I pretend you're fucking me on a crowded beach. When you say you like me. When you say you wouldn't trade this moment for all the cocaine in Hollywood. When I hear your father's rifles leaning up against the wall. When I've heard it all before. When silence. When I run.

Elegy

I am scrolling
through a dating app
at a funeral.
What I really want
is for the family
dog to take me
to the park
& throw me
a stick.
I rely entirely
on my horoscope
to justify
my bad behavior.
It's okay
to walk away.

Girl of My Dream

It's raining tomato sauce & meatballs. It's raining the lightning bolts kids cut out, little zigzags made of yellow construction paper. I'm the helicopter pilot in this storm & you're the girl I rescued from the tallest tower of a castle on fire. You couldn't jump out the window because the moat surrounding the castle was filled with pink catfish who had the heads of dragons & shot rings of fire into the sky with every swish of their fins. You've been waiting for me all along. I know this because of the way our shoulders touch. It isn't just the smallness of this helicopter. Picture this helicopter not as a helicopter but as the buoyancy of two lemons in an iced tea & our hearts are those lemons. I kiss you. I eat aluminum spaghetti & offer you some. You say okay. You say it might hurt but you can't resist it. We stick our plates out the window for some toppings. The lightning bolts taste like cheese. We drink beer on tap & it gets easier. When the sunset reminds you of fire, I am the firefighter. I turn on a siren to warn you, but it's no use.

The Right Things

I eat a half dozen Funfetti cupcakes
& then one more
because I cheat on my diet

& I cheat on my girlfriend
in my imagination
only in my imagination
so far only in my imagination

I give the bro in the left turn lane
the middle finger when he cuts me off
because it feels so good to do it
to yell *douchebag* but not be heard
though my gut says that's childish
& my guilt is immediate

If desire is weakness

If desire is pain
my knees are bruised
from running
from falling
down the hill
to an open-armed father
who is not really my father
but an old idea of my father

in which he does not criticize
my fade or my bowties

If pain is weakness
leaving the body

what good is the body
what good is the body

standing steady like a home

what is home

what good is the body
that cannot learn
from its wrongs
how real is the body
that does not torture itself
in attempts to heal
that does not still listen to the mixtape
of six summers ago
upon leaving
or having been left

wondering what is the right thing
in a world full of right things
growing out of wrong things
with the ferocity of dandelions

untamed & shooting
through the middle of everything

Selfie With a Dying Cat

I'm at the vet with my roommate while her cat is dying behind a few sets of closed doors, & I notice the purple paint on my flip-flops, which has not faded, which I'm looking down at because this is just too sad. I have nowhere to look but down. It's avoidance. It's reverence. It's something else entirely. The paint is the one you chose for the bathroom in the apartment we last lived in together. I painted that entire apartment because you were teaching summer school. Except for the bathroom. You painted the bathroom. It was a Saturday. You were painting the bathroom that purple while I was writing poems about how sad we'd become. How we began to turn on the TV during dinner & wear sports bras to bed. There's this way you stop & start missing something at the exact same moment. Scratching the paint off my flip-flops with my keys does no good. My roommate's cat is still dying & my roommate will still chain-smoke on the bench outside when it's over, while we choke on our memories of Kiddo, & I will always know where the paint was. We held on tight but these soft girl hands burned & burned.

Elegy

For Fred
July 2, 1956-December 24, 2012
& For Caitlin

I. *the last Father's Day your dad was alive*

I paid the tab for the three of us
        at the Vandalia Red Lobster
where he hit on the waitress
while we ate a basket of Cheddar Bay biscuits
& you held my hand under the table
laid your head on my shoulder
what a picture I thought
what a family.
When his cod came
he ate like a bird
same as you
swirling the white flakes around on his plate
more interested
        in his Maker's Mark on the rocks

II. *the next time we saw him*

he was drunk
& the time after that
& the time after that
he often was

but never in a scary way
just a man who needed to unwind
          after everything
though he often unraveled
faulty cassette
each time fear bubbling in our chests
          that the harm could be permanent
that one of these days
          Fred just might not work right again
we stopped over late one Friday night
& he described to us
in front of his girlfriend
Jack in hand
the glow-in-the-dark condoms
          he had recently bought
how his dick was a lightsaber
whoosh whoosh

III. *at Christmas a vodka buzz*

he threw a fit about the snow blower
we pitched in for with your sisters
cursing the weather
the Home Depot
himself
while your little nieces followed him around
          like ducklings
the three of you sent him home
where I imagine he drank
          himself into the darkest place
maybe the space between the wall & his gun cabinets

the slit in his mattress
beneath the facedown sides of the coins
        scattered across his kitchen counter

IV. *the next Christmas he was dead*

found in his living room
Christmas Eve morning
a nightmare so unreal
like it could only happen to someone in a movie
that that someone could leave the set
        & her staged sorrow behind
like she did the cloud of cigarette smoke
        outside her trailer
when she left for the day
when rehearsal was over

V. *that winter we stretched our happiness as best we could*

the muscles of it hyperextending until they snapped
the wells of our kindness toward each other
        ran dry daily
yet we clung to each other in the night
on your sister's living room floor
so deeply afraid of our grief
how it would manifest
how lazily I washed the colander
how you kissed me different
less
how it would ruin us

VI. *all week the funeral*

& the things that go with them
casket selections
photo slideshows
distant relatives
finger sandwiches
all we could do at the end of it
            was what Fred would've done
barhop Tipp City's golden triangle
slam whiskey shots
not to feed our burning
but to light even the smallest spark
            of happiness we could find
a mint antique car out in the parking lot
a morning in which we wake up having forgotten

VII. *as I make my way through the liquor store*

I walk down the whiskey aisle
not because I drink it
but because of how the light reflects here
neat arrangement of bottles all touching
the brown liquor golden

VIII. *I miss driving his Silverado to the drive-thru*

or home for him when he couldn't
miss the smell of Tide in the laundry room entryway
            in his house on Bowman

that somehow washed him clean of liquor
when he slipped on a freshly-ironed button-down
kissed my cheek
like I was home

Your Pinterest Board Called Wedding

I swear that's your actual finger: so
you want an oval engagement ring: my grief
circling around: coming back as a bird:
as a wing: fragile as the inner ear:
my alabaster heart: you: lace
everything: sleeves of your dress: lingerie: twitch
of my thigh: now you will marry a man: I don't know
his name: twitch in my eye: when we were
together: we made words: *let's get married*: our idea
of save the dates: Scrabble tiles: getting
married: back of your dress wide open: your finch
tattoo bursting through: my grief flying out
the window of you: what you like
about the finch: it always returns home

111.

Sara Tell Me Everything

tell me all about you / Sara tell me everything / how the corn stalks in your hometown lean to the left / even in summer's dead heat / tell me about the time your mom hugged Willie Nelson at the Jamboree / what our lives will be like / if we are sitting under this same tree a year from now / dear Sara / one day we'll go to Mexico together / swim in the cenote we watched so many YouTube videos about / where the teal water shimmers like wet nail polish / dear Sara / our first swim this summer in the Allegheny River & it's only April / we pack our lunches / peanut butter sandwiches / your favorite cheese-stuffed pretzel from the Sheetz up the road / melted Hershey bars / you put my fingers in your mouth / I run my tongue along your collarbone / I have the sudden urge to tell you everything / dear Sara / the best way to tell you anything / is to tear off the labels of our beer bottles & make a picture / here is Ohio / here is Cincinnati / Howell Avenue / your apartment / here are my shoes on your welcome mat / my keys on your counter / your hand on my cheek / dear Sara / I will write you a letter every week in September / I will take a shot of Knob Creek with you in Tennessee / & not make a face / dear Sara / let's get to know each other again & again / go back to Manhattan for another February / fumble with my button-fly / stomp our feet in the slush / no extra socks / here is where you ate pizza in college with your last four dollars / here on this bench is where you made one friend / where you left this town for that one / dear Sara / there is right now / our soft hands / my backseat / dear Sara / there is tomorrow & the day after that

Selfie at the Symphony

How can a string instrument whistle or something like a whistle? What if my mouth were full of strings like an instrument? You'd hold my neck so gently like I'm alive & I am. I'm not going to make a metaphor about how you can play me or say anything else about how you might touch me if I were an instrument. I love you. I got your name tattooed across my knuckles. I set my hand on top of the program & take a picture of it & send it to you. The people here are old with combed hair & are nothing like you. I've never seen a mandolin in real life until today. The way that guy moves his fingers must please some lover of his. A mandolin & a vagina are different. I write about sex a lot because I think about sex a lot not because I'm having it a lot but because I have sex with you & you live far away & I think about having sex with you when I'm not which is a lot. In the program I keep seeing the word *allegro*. I don't know what an allegro is but I know what Allegra is. I have some problems & one of them is allergies. I look up *allegro* when I get home. A measure of tempo. 120-168 beats per minute. My allegro heart for you, tattooed on my pinky knuckle following your name. Here is where I play you something with my mouth, where my heart earns its keep.

Tell Me We'll Never Get Used to It

I smile at you for hours & so do the Tiki men
because you're the prettiest girl
in this weird riverfront bar.
We have the best sex after the show
& it's intimate as hell—
little bedside lamp you touch to turn on,
our little eyelashes, the flannel sheets
in your best friend's attic with a little cat inside,
little monsters we invent, little sparks in our breath.
A little's enough. What it means to write stories
with skin. Your bare hands. My god. This is the night
we run out of nothing but breath,
the night we run miles with our mouths.

Long Distance Relationship

Start your car & cut the brakes. Don't worry about the traffic or the snow. You can slide the 322 miles from Cincinnati to Blacksburg. I'll stand outside. I'll stand on the corner of Eakin & Main. I'll throw my head back, grab my thigh at the thought of you. I'll throw my giant heart out into the street to stop your car. People will think there's been an accident. My heart all over the place, like always. This is no accident. There is no such thing as an accident. Do you believe in fate? Every fortune cookie I ever opened came true. *The love of your life will appear in front of you unexpectedly!* Once we sat in a room together on the first day of school. It was 8:00 AM & I was drinking orange juice & you had a big unicorn tattoo on your arm. Do you believe in love at first sight? Me neither. Years later we're on barstools, facing each other, your hands on my knees. Do you believe in love at first touch? *Love is like war: easy to begin but hard to stop.* We touched. In the middle of every day the sun hangs around you like halos. I am on my knees, waiting, Sara. I will know when you're almost here by the lilac in the air, despite the winter. I'll wash your car upon arrival, clean up my heart. I will build you a palace made of 100% tenderness, the kind found at hospitals among the baby cuddlers or the kind that fuels news stories where someone's dog rescued her from drowning. You will have a sunroom with a hammock. A Jacuzzi & a puppy. I will turn down the sheets & invite you.

There Is a Newness to the Best Things that Cannot Be Excelled

Don't we all just want that little spot in the sun
the one that shoots its way in through the blinds uninvited
there are studies about the sun & serotonin & feeling good
I tell my cats on the way out the door
remember to lie in the sun today
& they do remember
seems like an instinct for them to want to be warm
& now they are happier
more confident in their abilities to capture my shoelaces
sleep soundly for eighteen hours a day
lick each other's wounds until there is no need for me at all
when I look at the cats
there on my apartment floor or on my bookshelf
I pretend that the only sign of you is not the picture of us
they knock down with their tails
& I guess this is the part that we all knew was coming
see how I tried to not write a love poem but here it comes
here you are in my poem again
& I like that about you
how you show up in my poem
it's almost as if you show up in Virginia
I am in Virginia writing a poem you are in
so you are in Virginia too
you are wherever I am in a way that is similar to
a traditional view of some sort of goddess
that that goddess who is you

is omniscient or omni-present or whatever the word is
once we ballroom danced in the backyard
in our bikinis after the stereo broke
kept time with the chirps of the birds
& the squirrels hopping up the trees
drank two beers each
& spent the day dizzy over everything
once our foreheads touched for the very first time
& at that moment all of my guts turned into lungs
then all of my lungs turned into balloons
tonight I'm floating home to you

On Coming Home

Domesticity is all of our pets together in one room
plus me in my plaid pajama pants & you in no pants.
When you walk in the door, you take off your shoes
& then, right away, your pants because pants equals work

& this is not work, though there's cat litter stuck to your feet.
There're someone's dirty socks on the floor again.
There's the floor mat our guests rarely wipe their feet on.
So the cats scratch it up. So the dogs nap there.

There's the third time your mom doesn't show up
for Sunday breakfast & the tenth time
your sister tells you to please stop talking
about anything related to sex. I want to

fit in with the women in your family
but I am too reliable. You can count on me
to wink at you from across the bar ten years from now.
What if every time was like the first time?

By which I mean our lovemaking brings us
to tears in a stranger's bedroom & we don't know
when we'll see each other again, don't know
how the sun can shine when it's been cloudy for weeks.

Just know that I am a garden of boomerangs.
& Ingrid Michaelson is singing all the while.
I listened to that song again where the girl can't help
falling in love as a reminder that television is not

a stand-in for affection & neither is the bowl of cereal
one of us silently pours the other. Once I mailed you
a postcard from the mailbox down the street
which is to say my gratitude is the longest day of the year.

I make you promises but don't say them out loud.
Instead of marriage, matching heart tattoos
on our pointer fingers, a six-pack of Sierra Nevada
in the fridge, a homemade pizza. So much of love

is consumption. So much of my appetite is bottomless.
I've been running. & for once it isn't away.

How to Be Happy

If I give you the little turtle I found near the river
it means a lot more than the story I could tell you about it.

If I ask if you remember going down on me
in the neighbor's garage that one night in July

when you were wearing that black & white polka-dotted dress
& I was wearing that black & white polka-dotted bow tie

it means you are the spotlight of my nightly Etch A Sketch drawings.
When you wore those butterfly wings on Halloween

all I saw was angels. When I do the dishes
I am happy not because I love doing the dishes

but because you thank me every single time.

I've Avoided Sentimental Until Right This Second

I have embroidered your initials
on your side of my bed. I did it
in my best cursive & your favorite
shade of blue. This spot is yours
& tonight it's the only place for you.
I want you to go to this party I'm going to.
I want to kiss you up against the wall
but not drunkenly. I want us
to take the train somewhere.
I want us to take the train
to an amusement park. I want to ride
the Ferris wheel with you
even though I'm afraid of heights.
I want everything to go wrong
by which I mean I want us to get stuck
at the top for hours & speculate
about controversial ideas like was Jesus
a virgin & the best way to train a puppy.
I want you to be the girl
version of Johnny Appleseed.
Janie Appleseed. I want you
to eat apples & plant the seeds
from the apples you ate.
The trees will grow to the moon
& so I will take my first & last trip
to space one warm day in April.

I will become an astronaut for a day.

My childhood space camp dreams are coming true.

Your apple trees will sustain us forever.

Lana Del Rey Concert, Noblesville, Indiana

Hold a 24 oz. beer can to your ear
& that's the nearest ocean. Hold back
your excitement, toss your hair over one shoulder
& that's foreplay. You wanted to get all dressed up
so you did — red lipstick, cat eyes, black tights.
I try to match my breathing to Lana's swaying hips,
to the red & white collar creeping up her candy throat.
I want to feel the sun go down in my hamstrings first.
My body a pulley, a sunset, a stone.
There are so many great white moons in this night.
I can see down your shirt a little, even after dark.

Poem in Which Our Breakup Isn't So Bad

When you asked me *do you think it's possible*
to OD on holy basil & I said *should we try*
call that team effort. When our phones light up

call that grieving, call that light
at the end of the tunnel. We look right into it.
We cannot afford to worry about our vision.

We remind each other where we put our microscopes
& have seen almost everything up close—
holes we never spackled, hair thick in the drain,

opposite ends of betrayal. We have determined
both feel bad. We spend time together now
but mostly we spend time apart. When it hurts

we say it hurts. We say that a lot. When we tell the truth
the light changes. When we tell the truth we don't worry
about what we are looking for, what we might find.

Barter

In the beginning, that summer,
I kept a tally, starred the days on my calendar
we spent kissing, those days somehow

the next days. Those stars a map far away.
The next days. There are galaxies inside of us
we cannot access. There is no telescope

in this house. Basic breakup questions: How
did we get here? Where are we going?
We decide I will not sleep in the guest room.

You are still nice to me. You buzz my head
in the bathroom on a rainy day
in exchange for a six pack of Sierra Nevada.

You drink all six. You press
your palm against my head,
fold my ear out of the way of the clippers,

first time we've touched in weeks.
Last summer, on the porch, mid-haircut,
you told me that buzzing my head

was the gayest you'd ever felt.
Someday you might cut a man's hair.
You might run your hands through his beard.

Moving Out

When we begin to divide up the house, we look closely
at the silverware. Months will pass before either of us know
what to do with our mouths. We try to keep our sadness
from setting in, sit at the kitchen table together,
google *best dating apps for lesbians*, both of us afraid
the next person you will sleep with will be a man.
When I ask why you want to sleep with one,
you say *how I want to be mistreated is cultural*.
The apples in the fruit bowl shine like they are not even real.
From here, it is impossible to see their bruises.

Anniversary

Monogamy is not a dominant trait, is not
scattered like handfuls of birdseed.
My parents have been married for thirty-three years today.
I built a birdhouse with my dad when I was nine.
It has housed one thousand birds.
Others flew into our window, died on impact.
I dug holes for them, picked dandelions,
my sadness exploding in the backyard. Tires spinning
in the mud. There are so many kinds of dying
& even more kinds of tenderness.
None of my grief has grown wings.
Tires spinning in the mud. You have this bird
tattoo on your chest, same as your mother's.
I could say her name a thousand times.

On Coming Home

I finally fit in   with the women in your family

        can't be counted on   can't keep a promise

tattoo here to remind me   I gave that up   traded it

        & the barking dogs   for the silence

I thought I wanted   I am in my little apartment still

        wearing my plaid pajama pants   still

stepping in cat litter   this may still be true

        ten years later   if my cats live forever

ten years from now   we will not

        be in the same bar   we've broken up

we've sobered up   tattoo is here   to remind me

        this is not a ring   I can

just slip off my finger   one old feeling

still the same   we don't know

when we'll see   each other again

          don't know how the sun   can shine

when it's been   cloudy   for weeks

          if I can still be   considered

a garden   call me barren   call me   dirt

          call me   dead   to you   call me

tomorrow   on the phone   remind me

          how I've hurt you

give me   what   I deserve   what can I grow now

          I have given up   on boomerangs

what I throw away   will never come back

          I have given up   on the USPS

nine times out of ten   I cry   when I so much as look

          at a mailbox   Ingrid Michaelson sings & sings

I am the girl   who can't help   what I can't

help   everything   nothing   I have to eat

my pizza   pre-made   a cliché   who cannot

cook for herself   it's so sad   what if

all I am   is someone   who hurts   from hurting

someone   who hurts from hurting

someone who hurts

if anyone is asking   yes   I am still running

training for a marathon   in fact   Sara

you predicted   which way   I'd run

pointed to it   every direction   away

How many times sorry has not mattered

is what I think about every time I am sorry.
How many rooms have I cried in this year?

How many gallon jugs could I fill with tears?
What is an ocean if not a burn?

Cover myself in aloe or drink it but everything
still hurts. When my heart is broken I say nothing

to my father, who will never know because he never asks.
He will not ask why I am here

by myself this Christmas. He does not understand
my kind of love or even his own kind.

At the bus stop I yell I *love you*
to no one in particular. I feel my feelings

& it's one thing I'm not sorry for.
Every holiday card I get this winter

still has her name on it.

Ars Poetica

i won't get used to eating / at this little table / across from no one / across from
a gray wall / across from a blender & mixing bowls on a shelf / i sit here & look
around for a while / before i get any food out / at the clock shaped like ohio /
the to-do list / the coat rack / & try to feel proud of something / not my roots
/ not the way i walk / away / but my bike helmet / hanging there / evidence / i
can move my body in a new way / i take risks / sort of / you can die on a bike
you know / people text while driving / people leave because they think / there
might be something better / my cats meow by now / dinnertime / their hunger
so physiological / so unlike mine / sometimes i want a person who does not
want me back / sometimes i am the wanted person / mostly i am the person
who has everything / but not now / i took that for granted / so much of my life
spent / not needing / nothing to hunger for / for so long i have been paired up
/ with the sunsets of people / blooming roses on the first warm day of people /
& when i wreck it / i always wreck it / it's never a train off the rails / it's unseen
internal damage / the carbon monoxide detector that doesn't work / but you
only know / when it's too late / when you're dead inside / dead literally / train
won't explode but will stop suddenly / will ruin everything / when i'm lonely /
i put all this stake in being wanted / like never before / like if i could open me
up / look right into my chest / what would i find / besides the sound / of metal
on metal / heart sometimes untraceable / heart most times too big / say i bleed
out / what if i said my sins out loud / could be / my own therapist / my own
safe space / say it lisa / say what you've done / walked away from / given up on /
held the face / of everyone you've ever kissed / sweet grapefruit of the morning
/ told the truth / told her everything / say ohio was the last place i was happy /
said ohio is the place i said / over & over / i will never go back to / the blood there
means nothing / say i make a life somewhere else / say i still have you / somehow

I'll admit, we were everything

I ever wanted to make. Our hands
on each other always the same,
a soft, slow science. Is anything immune

to ruin? Candle not a candle
when you light it & forget it.
Umbrella out in the storm

& the wind. We split, years ago now,
everything halved, the silverware,
open bags of sugar, two pets each.

When one of the cats died last week, the sorry
for your loss card from the vet
addressed to us both. Some things are forever

because the world cannot keep
track of every ending. I have kept you
permanent on purpose, your poems

in my backpack, your hair, not in my drain
but when I clean it, I think of the way
your hair sat in ours, intimacy up-close.

You have found your person
& mine is just an idea. But I know
I'll lie with her in any patch of grass at dusk

& be able to know the moon. From anywhere.
Isn't that amazing? My therapist says live
in the present because I'm stuck

in the past & always looking
ahead, can speak only in the conditional
because I'm hopeful, speculate

about how to acquire a love that moves
room to room in the house I'll share with someone.
I'll admit I'm still drawn to the heat of fire,

approach it like I've never been burned,
step closer & closer, no word for the moment
between when it feels good & it's too late.

At your father's funeral

it's different no dead body & I am not anyone's girlfriend mid-afternoon
mid-April spring is late this year like every year another dead dad yours on
his couch his beers or his heart in his sleep I think of Fred my guilt immediate
& long winded my guilt Caitlin I went through the motions held her hand
but dropped it left our apartment left her a note left Ohio I leave work early
leave the city to get to the service two hours north Oil City not a city at all no
bike lanes no bus lines only lines of coke & lines out church doors on Sundays
I pass the corner store think of the bait & the grape cigarellos we'd pick up
for your dad those long weekend days we'd drive the mud road between your
dad's place & your mom's stop halfway & fuck in the car loved each other so
hard we'd cry in the leather seat's sunspot today your girlfriend is with you
she will do the work I excused myself from when I pull up to the funeral
home the neighborhood is outside smoking when I go inside & see you in
front of the urn I crack open cry for the hour & then some when I hug you
I hold you our arms the same arms they always were eventually a church
person says things but I don't know what I just think of your dad how he
neither liked nor disliked me my discomfort his discomfort his confusion
how I am unlike other women but also not a boy not equipped to give him
grandkids still he opened his house to us beers & the three of us sharing a
Marie Callender mixed berry pie whole nights in front of the TV he'd fall
asleep on the couch his way of giving us the bed

It's Your Birthday & This Year I Am Not Sad

Leo season, hot & sticky & we are
sweetly self-involved, two fire signs
still working on our friendship, as in, finally,
the work is working, as in, finally, I can say
I love you & it doesn't trigger betrayal,
empty hands in empty apartments.
I take you for Thai, Smiling Banana Leaf,
a place we never went to when we were together,
this new vegan paradise somehow
a windshield finally clear after the salt of winter,
crystal. We get our usual— me, the kee mao,
you, the basil eggplant.
Your birthday dinner last year,
only Ethiopian place in town, first time I had to
see you with someone else. I had to cry
the two-mile walk home & the next day
& the next day, had to delete my Tinder profile,
suddenly understood my grief,
not just a weight but an anchor,
& I was paralyzed, could give nothing
to anyone, not even myself. *Time heals*
all wounds, yes, but time the wound
& picked scab long before the salve.
We can go thrift shopping & for long walks
at the reservoir. We can have girlfriends
who are not each other & for this

I credit not just time but our therapists.
After dinner we walk the dogs, the chore
I hated the most when we lived together—
their barks, how they'd bite each other
when they'd see another dog,
how you weren't ever home to do it yourself.
My cats ate your books & puked on your rugs.
You never got mad. What can I say
about space except that I needed it.
I live in silence now & it's exactly what I want—
I had to learn that. Your girlfriend calls us on our walk,
asks if we want to get ice cream.
It's not the first time she buys me ice cream
& won't be the last. She & I talk about the right kind
of running shoes & the right kind of pizza.
We talk about our cute mutual friends & you remind us
it's your birthday. We tell you you're hot.
We wash our sticky hands & walk home.
When you hug me, you hold me,
but not like I'm leaving.

Notes

"Like the number of times I stub my toe" in "Always a Man" is language taken from Rachael Shockey from a conversation we had on sexual assault & its coverage in the media.

"The Place Where I Again Think of You" takes its title from a line in Kenneth Koch's poem, "To You."

"There Is a Newness to the Best Things That Cannot Be Excelled" takes its title from a line in Dorothea's Lasky's poem, "On Old Ideas."

"Tell Me We'll Never Get Used to It" takes its title from the last line in Richard Siken's poem, "Scheherazade."

"I'll admit, we were everything" takes its title & the rest of the first sentence from Shelby Vane.

Acknowledgments

Thank you to the editors of the following journals for giving these poems, often in alternate versions, & sometimes under different titles, their first homes: *bedfellows*, *Bettering American Poetry Anthology* (Vol. 2), *Bone Bouquet*, *Cosmonauts Avenue*, *Fourth River*, *Ghost Town*, *Juked*, *Lambda Literary*, *Open Arts Forum*, *Pittsburgh Poetry Review*, *Rattle*, *Revolution House*, *Salt Hill*, *Smartish Pace*, *South Carolina Review*, *Sundog Lit*, *Tampa Review*, *Tar River Poetry*, *Tinderbox Poetry Journal*, *Trnsfr*, *Two Hawks Quarterly*, *Vinyl Poetry*, *Waxwing*, & *Word Riot*.

Thank you to the MFA program at Virginia Tech for three years of good thinking and writing. Thank you Matty Bennett, Emily Dhatt, Xandria Phillips, & Nora Salem. Thank you Jeff Mann, Erika Meitner, & especially Bob Hicok.

I talk a lot of shit about Cincinnati for a lot of reasons, but I had some of the very best teachers there. Thank you Don Bogen, Kimberly Campanello, Danielle Deulen, Kristi Maxwell, and Kate Mitchell. A very special thank you & all my love to Erica Dawson.

Thank you Caitlin Vagedes.

Thank you Leah Addison for always cheering me on.

Thank you Kamal Kimball for thinking with me & writing poems with me & being a sad boi with me.

Thank you Rochelle Hurt, Julia Koets, & Rachael Shockey for taking first looks at this book & for your very sweet friendship.

Thank you Shelby Vane for reading this thing. Thank you for your poems & for your ferocious tenderness.

Thank you Lynn Melnick for your poems, tweets, smart edits, & encouragement.

Thank you YesYes Books. Thank you Alban Fischer. Thank you especially KMA Sullivan for the time, generosity, enthusiasm, & kindness that nurtured this book. Thank you for believing.

Thank you to my parents—to my mom, best example of compassion & kindness there is, & to my dad, for teaching me to persevere. You've both shaped me.

Thank you to my chosen family in Pittsburgh: Annah Darling, Jane Hartung, Sarah Najjar, & Angela Wiley. Couldn't do life without y'all & wouldn't want to.

Thank you to my girlfriend, Micaela Corn, for the attention, care, & enthusiasm you give to your poems & to mine. Your sweetness carries me through the darkest days.

Thank you, most of all, Sara Watson, for your editorial eye, your poems, your patience, & your friendship. We never stopped laughing.

Also from YesYes Books

RECENT CHAPBOOK COLLECTIONS

Vinyl 45s

 Inside My Electric City by Caylin Capra-Thomas

 Exit Pastoral by Aidan Forster

 Of Darkness and Tumbling by Mónica Gomery

 The Porch (As Sanctuary) by Jae Nichelle

 Juned by Jenn Marie Nunes

 Unmonstrous by John Allen Taylor

 Preparing the Body by Norma Liliana Valdez

 Giantess by Emily Vizzo

Blue Note Editions

 Beastgirl & Other Origin Myths by Elizabeth Acevedo

 Kissing Caskets by Mahogany L. Browne

 One Above One Below: Positions & Lamentations by Gala Mukomolova

Companion Series

 Inadequate Grave by Brandon Courtney

 The Rest of the Body by Jay Deshpande

www.ingramcontent.com/pod-product-compliance
Lightning Source LLC
Chambersburg PA
CBHW060429090426
42734CB00011B/2505